Releasing The Inner Voice

A Guide For Singers

MARJORIE HALBERT

Published by ISI Publishing
Brentwood, Tennessee

Copyright © 1996 by Marjorie Halbert

Second Edition 2007

Library of Congress Cataloging-in-Publication Data

Halbert, Marjorie

Releasing The Inner Voice, A Guide For Singers

Library of Congress Catalog Card Number: 96-75598

ISI Publishing, PO Box 431, Brentwood, TN 37027-0431
A division of Impact Seminars, Inc.

Printing Number:
10 9 8 7 6 5 4 3 2

ISBN 0-9630968-2-6

This book is dedicated to voice teachers, coaches, and students who inspire each other to create beautiful singing.

A personal note...

Students and teachers of singing, possess a great gift. They are touched by the power of music and the undeniable desire to reach beyond conventional forms of expression and communication. Yet, all singers have experienced hesitation in expressing the art that lives within.

Every voice has an innate wisdom. All of us have the ability and knowledge to sing freely and expressively, but many times we stop the natural process by over manipulating or straining to control the sound. Because of the anxious desire to *do it right,* often singers do too much. Learning to *relax* the body and *allowing* it to sing is the foundation for releasing the inner voice.

Gaining this wisdom and experience does not come easily. Singers need trusted guides to help focus attention on positive, energized ideas that liberate the voice — guides who will recognize the spiritual dimension of the art and nurture the love of music.

My goal throughout this book is to help the reader find the balance between learned technique and inner wisdom. Combining the two with intellectual curiosity and disciplined practice will result in singing that is truly inspired. If we can achieve this goal, we will have found a way to give ourselves to the art of singing and music will live through us!

To John

My gratitude for his caring and believing — for his encouragement and tireless energy to complete this book.

Acknowledgements

For contributing time and talent:

Christy Halbert, Jonathan Riggs, Ellen Sims, Suzanne Matheny, Barbara Halbert, Matthew Collins, Anne Craig, Mary Shambarger, Emma Lee Stobaugh, Karen Lee Turner, and Kristi Whitten.

Special thanks to:

Mark Courey, M.D., Professor of Otolaryngology at the University of California, San Francisco, Department of Otolaryngology – Head and Neck Surgery.

Medical Illustrator: Dominic Doyle

Music is your own experience, your thoughts, your wisdom. If you don't live it, it won't come out your horn.

—Charlie Parker

If you are a beginning voice student, this guide will serve as a foundation for effective voice training. If you are an experienced singer, ***Releasing the Inner Voice*** will offer reminders and a challenge to be consistent. Training the voice is a life-long endeavor; it requires discipline, concentration and patience as your voice develops. It is fascinating to hear how the voice changes as you build upon the fundamental precepts of sound vocal technique. To sing with confidence and self-assurance and to use the voice most effectively requires learning about the physiological and psychological aspects of singing.

Realizing that voices need time for growth, the best gift that singers can give themselves is attentiveness to the complex components of vocal technique, consistent practice, and thoughtful preparation for studying voice. This guide is designed to assist in discovering and applying some of the elements of the study of singing.

Topics and Sections

The questions, check lists, and thoughts on the even numbered pages are designed to encourage you to continually evaluate personal practice habits, reflect on what you are reading, and collect questions and concerns to discuss with your teacher or coach. Dating your comments will also indicate your progress as you become the singer you desire to be.

Use the even numbered pages to...

collect **questions and concerns,**
reflect **on what you are learning,**
note **discoveries important to you, and**
commit **to practice what you are learning.**

An Overview

Following the description of correct **posture** for singing is a section of **breathing exercises** to help locate the muscles used for proper breathing for singers. It is important to establish a strong foundation for effective breath management since the breath initiates and sustains the tone. The **terms and definitions** included in this guide are words commonly used to communicate concepts and technical aspects of singing. These quick reference phrases should assist you in beginning your own research into these and other pedagogical terms.

Maintaining a healthy voice is vital for everyone; including students training for performance careers, people who enjoy singing in choirs, children's choir leaders, and professional speakers. In this section questions concerning vocal hygiene are addressed. And, since no one is immune to illness, learning **how to cope with sickness** is helpful when your voice is affected by colds, allergies or infection.

A common question raised by every student is, **"how should I practice"** or "how can I improve practicing?" A well thought out plan of action for every practice session will result in better use of time and a more productive session. Use the vocalises and practice guides to establish well-disciplined techniques for effective practice sessions.

The last section includes a list of **vocalises** which are designed for maintaining and building the voice. These short, basic, vocal exercises are to be sung throughout the vocal range and utilized to enhance performance techniques. It is just as important to exercise the voice and the muscles involved as it is for a runner to stretch her/his muscles before running a race, and it is best to be completely independent when vocalizing and learning vocal literature. While playing the piano is preferred, many people find that working with recorded accompaniment on occasion is beneficial. An accompaniment CD for the vocalizes is available as an additional aid to individual practice so you can become self reliance in this process; it is designed to assist those who find that using the piano is awkward or impractical. Use these tools to become a student of the art and structure of singing.

Releasing The Inner Voice

will benefit you most if you are willing to…

✓ take notes as you read the guide and practice

✓ use the even numbered pages to communicate with your teacher

✓ consistently follow the guided activities throughout the book

✓ complete and follow your schedule for practice

✓ complete practice sheets daily

✓ follow your practice plan

✓ write evaluations of practice sessions

The **practice sheets** at the end of this guide will act as daily reminders of your commitment to consistent practice. It is helpful to record questions and comments about technique, literature, vocal problems, and accomplishments to review with your teacher or coach. An effective way of measuring progress is by maintaining accurate records following each session.

Information in this guide will complement your voice lessons. By referring to the guide extensively during daily practice times, you may find that it becomes a *how to* manual in establishing a daily routine of vocal study.

Vocal development is up to you – applying the necessary ingredients to make
positive changes in your singing is a matter of discipline, desire,
and dedication. Follow a practice plan and commit yourself to
the essential steps toward developing your voice and
you will see and hear immediate results.

Check the posture habits that apply to you. Decide to change unchecked habits and refer to this list as you continue to improve your posture.

☑ I avoid carrying heavy book bags over one shoulder

❑ I seldom slump at my desk

❑ I consistently maintain my shoulders comfortably back

❑ I seldom stand with weight on one leg

❑ My chin does not protrude during singing or speaking

☑ I avoid looking down when standing or walking

❑ I keep my shoulders even and relaxed

☑ I avoid standing swayback

❑ I am aware of my posture

❑ I begin every practice session with correct posture

Posture

*Correct posture is the first step
in producing a beautiful tone*

Everyone has their own style of standing, sitting, and walking. We move from one activity or task to another without thinking of aligning the body because attention is on the action. Rarely do we concentrate on correct posture unless a teacher or friend brings it to our attention, or unless we happen to see ourselves in a mirror.

Posture reveals the subconscious. It is obvious when someone is depressed or excited, angry or joyful, because their body reflects their mood. Individual personalities become apparent in the way people carry themselves. These become posture habits: an individual's uniqueness showing through in the habitual ways he or she moves.

These habits are not typically examples of perfect posture. In fact, posture habits may be quite constricting, but because they have become so ingrained, even poor posture may feel normal or even comfortable. To prepare the body for singing, you must make a conscious effort to learn and maintain correct body alignment. Posture is the FIRST step in producing and supporting a beautiful tone.

Four Exercises to Improve Posture

Rag Doll

Bend the knees and lean over completely loose and limp, tipping the torso, and dropping the arms toward the floor. Slowly straighten the spine while remaining relaxed until correct posture is assumed. Repeat three times.

Diagonal Stretch

Lying on the floor on your back, extend your arms over your head. Stretch – alternating the stretch between right leg/left arm and left leg/right arm for four counts each. Repeat three times.

Back Against the Wall

Stand with feet together and heels against the wall. Without bending the knees or curving the shoulders forward, try pressing the small of the back against the wall. Some people find this exercise difficult. The goal is not to flatten the back; the goal is to tuck the hips and lengthen the spine. Step away from the wall and notice the body alignment. Inhale and exhale slowly two times, then repeat the entire exercise.

Ready to Sing

Stand tall, roll the shoulders backward in a complete circular movement three times, leaving the shoulders down, back and relaxed. Next, tip the crown of the head back slightly, then pull the chin down and back slightly to straighten the spine and lift the sternum. You should feel a buoyancy in the body and a little lift in the torso.

Learning Good Posture for Singing

*Standing tall with a feeling of readiness will
heighten your awareness of the performance.*

Practicing good posture for singing is most effective in front of a full length mirror. It is preferable to wear workout or dance clothing the first time you work on posture so you can see even the slightest muscular movement clearly.

❶ Stand tall. Feet should be about shoulder width apart (women may elect to stand with one foot slightly in front of the other), and weight evenly distributed on both legs. Legs should feel lengthened and the knees should never be locked. The correct stance should feel solid, balanced and comfortable.

❷ The torso should feel lifted and the chest comfortably high but never rigid. Shoulders should feel as though they form a suspended "T" with the spine and with arms relaxed down at your side. Guard against upper arms squeezing into the torso or shoulders raising toward the ears during singing.

❸ The position of the head and neck are extremely important! The chin should be parallel to the floor, the neck aligned with the spine (the chin should never protrude) and the top of the head should feel lifted so there is no chance of compressing the vertebrae of the neck. Balancing the weight of the head at the top of the spine is significant in alleviating tension in the neck and jaw.

In this position, roll both shoulders back in a complete circular motion four times leaving the shoulders down and comfortably relaxed. If the neck feels tense, tip the head forward dropping the chin close to the chest. Roll the head slowly toward the right, back to center then slowly toward the left before returning to center and lifting the head.

> *If you feel a particular spot of tension during this exercise, stop the rotation - inhale deeply then exhale as you relax the shoulders and lengthen the neck. This exercise should be done slowly and carefully to protect the neck.*

Now that you have achieved correct posture, the entire body should feel open, resilient, and ready for activity.

Description of my current posture habits...

Slouched ; Shoulders brought forward

Posture habits I would like to improve...

Everything

An excellent source of information and practical application toward balancing the body for efficiency is the Alexander Technique. You can find numerous books and articles about the Alexander Technique, and specialists who offer workshops and private lessons for those interested in studying this unique balanced approach to moving and aligning the body

CORRECT POSTURE

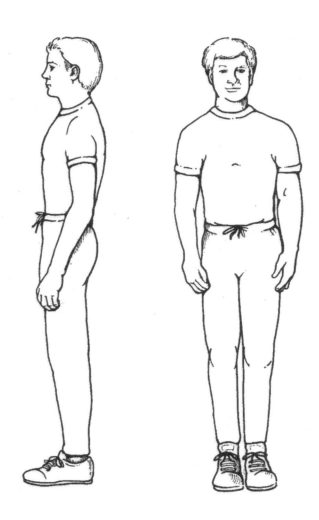

Once you have attained correct posture, you are ready to begin breathing exercises or vocalises. If this way of standing feels unusual or slightly rigid, keep practicing until it becomes more comfortable (listen to your body – if you feel too constricted, wait to work on posture with your teacher). Correcting poor posture habits takes time, and you should re-train the body slowly and deliberately. Note: The same correct upper torso posture should be used for sitting in choral rehearsals.

My breathing technique could best be described as…

a small breath that takes a long time to do

The most important underlying factor for producing a beautiful tone is correct breathing.

I need help with…

- *Posture*

- *breathing*

- *Relaxing the muscles in my jaw & throat*

Breathing for Singing

The most important underlying factor for producing a beautiful tone is correct breathing.

There have been hundreds of books written on vocal technique; and, through the years, there have probably been hundreds of differing opinions on how to manage the breath for singing. Thankfully, with the help of modern technology and devoted vocal pedagogues who have observed muscular activity in the vocal tract, thorax, and abdomen, this process has become more clearly defined; therefore, breath management is being taught with more consistency.

Most beginning voice students are not aware of the importance of learning a new or improved way of breathing. Breathing is habitual, natural and subconscious, so altering the process seems unnecessary. Many times the primary step in learning breath management and support for the tone is becoming conscious of the significance of the breath for singing.

The most important underlying factor for producing a beautiful tone is correct breathing! The breath **is** the tone. Without breath, there is no tone. If you want to sing throughout your lifetime, it is vital that you build a strong and secure foundation of vocal health and good singing habits. Building this foundation is the best way to insure against chronic vocal problems in the future. The fundamental tools of vocal technique are posture and breath. Any time you experience vocal difficulties, look first at the basics. Is your posture allowing the body to work properly? And, is your breath supporting the tone?

Breathing for singing is exactly the same for speaking, except that it is expanded. There are no tricks to learn nor is there a secret to managing the breath. Breathing for singing is a natural process.

The task for the singer is to learn to slow down the process of breathing and make it more deliberate.

During inhalation the position of my chest is usually…

Sucked in
(Sometimes)

To be self-aware is an important first step toward being receptive to a teacher's instruction on how to improve.

The movement of my abdominal muscles during inhalation is best described as…

During inhalation (or inspiration), the diaphragm (a double dome-shaped tendonous muscle separating the thorax from the abdominal cavity), flattens; at the same time, the ribs lift and separate, and air is drawn into the lungs because of a partial vacuum created in the lungs. Exhalation (or expiration) is the reverse action (refer to page 25 for action of the intercostals muscles). The diaphragm relaxes back into the double-dome position, the ribs drop slightly and move inward, and air is exhaled. The task for the singer is to learn to slow down the process of breathing and make it more deliberate. Sustaining a long phrase, singing with controlled dynamics, and supporting the tone are dependent upon training the muscles used in breathing.

> It is **absolutely necessary** to learn how to support the tone correctly so you will not constrict muscles in the throat and neck as you sing.

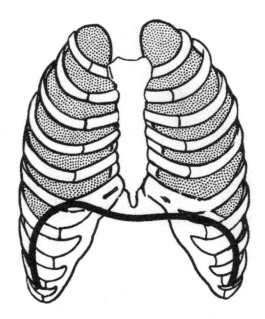 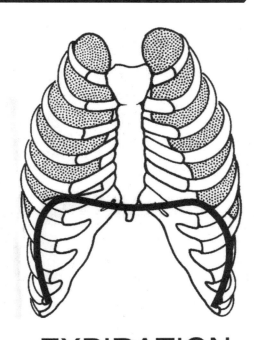

INSPIRATION   EXPIRATION
(the diaphragm descends)   *(the diaphragm rises)*

Heavy line indicates movement of the diaphragm.

Learning Correct Breathing Technique Is Important To A Singer Because Correct Breath Management...

- relaxes the throat.

- prepares the body for action.

- maintains energy.

- is the power source for singing.

- is the foundation for the tone.

- maintains the vocal line.

- assists in projection.

- assists in executing melismas.

- is primary to vocal health.

Breathing Exercises

*Remember that these exercises should feel
natural and comfortable to the body.*

Breathing exercises are significant in developing the voice because correct inhalation and exhalation are critical to proper support of the tone. It is imperative to establish good posture before beginning these exercises. Optimum progress takes place with optimum preparation. Learning proper breathing technique will create a strong foundation for singing that will last a lifetime!

Each exercise should feel natural, enabling and energizing the body. Breath should fill the lungs, not stuff the lungs! The breathing exercises described here will guide you to a natural rhythm of air flow and you will notice consistent muscular activity that will help maintain good breath management. Remember, these exercises should feel comfortable. If you experience discomfort, or if you find that your tendency is to "lock the breath" during an exercise, stop and wait for your next lesson to correct the difficulty with guidance from your teacher.

Always begin breathing exercises with good posture, relaxation, and "soft knees." Locking the knees inhibits circulation which will eventually affect the entire body. Whenever possible, do these exercises in front of a mirror. Checking progress is much easier when you can see what the body is doing.

1. Inhale slowly through the nose and exhale slowly through the mouth. The object is to feel as though you are smelling a beautiful fragrance during inhalation and slowly releasing the air on exhalation. Close your eyes and concentrate on the action of the rib cage and the abdominal wall. Notice that during inhalation the ribs are opening and lifting slightly and that the abdominal wall is expanding.

Repeat this slow, controlled inhalation and exhalation eight times. Make sure that you feel a natural expansion and a consistent and easy flow of air. Never try to force air into the lungs or "stuff" the lungs full of air. Inhalation should be silent (noisy inhalation is usually a sign of tension in the throat or neck). The throat should feel open without constricting or pulling. During exhalation, allow the expanded ribs to stay open as long as possible.

Before Beginning
Breathing Exercises
Remember To...

❑   Establish correct posture

❑   Observe movement of the abdominal muscles

❑   Allow the chest to remain comfortably high

❑   Align the head with the spine

❑   Control the release of air

❑   Feel poised and ready for action

❑   Inhale silently

❑   Avoid clavicular (high chest) breathing

❑   Open and relax the body

2. Inhale slowly through the nose while raising both arms overhead (notice the open feeling in the rib cage). Without straining or locking, suspend the breath for three seconds, then exhale through the mouth while lowering the arms. Maintain rib expansion as long as possible during the exhalation.

Repeat this exercise six times. Allow the ribs to remain open without forcing and make sure that the shoulders are relaxed down throughout the exercise. Suspending the breath for a few seconds after inhalation encourages the sensation of having adequate intake of air.

3. Inhale, then pant like a dog for five seconds. Observe the abdominal muscles working, contracting and releasing; then inhale and exhale freely to release the muscles.

Repeat the panting exercise four times — trying to keep abdominal muscles and breath moving evenly! Inhale and exhale freely between repetitions to release the muscles. At the beginning, the breath may be quite uneven, but keep trying — it will become more consistent with practice!

4. Inhale slowly through the nose and exhale with a hissing sound. Remember to expand the ribs and the abdominal wall upon inhalation and let the ribs stay open as long as they will during the hissing.

Repeat four times, increasing the exhalation three seconds with each repetition. You will immediately see the benefit of slowing the stream of air in order to control the exhalation. It is very important to allow expansion in the ribs without forcing.

5. Inhale slowly through the nose; then repeat the word "who" approximately ten times before taking another breath. Allow small puffs of air before the word.

Repeat four times relaxing between each set. This exercise should not be hurried.

6. Inhale slowly through the nose; then beginning on a relatively high note, sing an open vowel down the chromatic scale to your lowest pitch.

Repeat four times, concentrating on maintaining an open and lifted torso. Guard against letting the ribs contract quickly and the chest press downward during the exercise.

Observations and Notes

Additional Exercises

7. This is a modified breathing technique used in some yoga classes: With forefinger and thumb at the nose, close the left nostril and inhale slowly through the right nostril, then close the right nostril (opening the left), to exhale slowly.

Repeat three times; then repeat <u>three more times </u>reversing the sides for inhalation and exhalation.

8. Inhale slowly through the nose, open the mouth, and initiate five short puffs of air as though you are blowing out five candles.

Repeat ten times – remember to close the mouth before inhaling.

9. Inhale slowly through the nose concentrating on the expansion of the ribs; then repeat the ABC's as quickly as possible and as many times as possible. Relax and breathe freely before repeating.

Repeat this exercise three times. You will notice a difference in the number of times the ABC's can be repeated if the volume is quiet and the tempo is quick. Another factor in prolonging this exercise is allowing the ribs to stay out as long as possible.

10. Inhale slowly through the nose. Open the mouth and begin exhaling, then initiate a tone singing "ah" – choosing any note in the mid-range.

Repeat five times singing different pitches and prolonging the sustained tone with each repetition. You may also wish to try singing different vowel sounds.

Optimum progress takes place with optimum preparation!

The foundation
of effective
communication
is sharing
common
language.

Additional Terms

Research Notes

TERMS and DEFINITIONS

ABDOMEN
The abdomen is the region of the body that lies between the thorax and the pelvis; it encloses the internal organs in that area of the body. The abdominal wall is divided into posterior (back), lateral (sides) and anterior (front) walls. The frontal wall is divided into three regions:

> Epigastric – upper third just below the sternum
> Umbilical – central part of the abdominal wall
> Hypogastric – lower third of the abdominal region

ADAMS'S APPLE
The most forward part of the thyroid cartilage which is often visible as a slight protrusion below the chin in men.

APPOGGIO
Chest muscles, rib cage and side walls of the abdomen maintaining an open and suspended feeling during singing. There is no perceived collapse of the upper rib cage, even in recovery during rests in the music.

ARTICULATORS
The tongue, lips, cheeks, teeth, palate and jaw which work together to perform valving and shaping functions in the vocal tract to assist in forming vowels and consonants of speech and singing.

ASPIRATE
The sound *h* in English as in *help* that produces a slight puff of breath which interrupts the legato line, especially when singing an open vowel.

BEL CANTO
An Italian musical term meaning *beautiful singing*. It is the art of creating a beautiful vocal line with perfect evenness throughout the range, skillful legato and accomplished agility. Bel canto does not emphasize volume as much as flawless technique. This style of singing originated in Italy during the late 16th century reaching a pinnacle in the early 19th century when beauty of the vocal line was paramount.

Understanding and using common terms and definitions will allow you to communicate more effectively with your teacher, coach, accompanists and other singers.

Additional Terms

Research Notes

BELTING
In popular music, using the chest voice in the higher part of the vocal range rather than switching into head voice during singing. Modifying vowels for more open production is necessary to maintain relaxation in the throat as pitches rise. The soft palate is raised and vowels are usually sung brightly toward the front of the mouth in belt singing.

CHEST VOICE
The lower part of the vocal range and usually the register used in everyday speech. Perceived sensation in the body (created by sympathetic vibration) is often described as in the upper chest. When sung with balance and freedom, the chest voice can be described as rich and full. Some singers force the chest voice believing that the sound will be more powerful, but forcing is NOT necessary to enhance and amplify the tone. Let your voice teacher guide you in using chest voice singing.

CHIAROSCURO
This Italian word literally means *light and shadow*. A primary goal for singers is to find a balance of tone that is not too light/bright *(chiaro)* nor too dark/covered *(scuro)* to sing freely with the most beautifully resonant tone.

CLAVICLE
The collar bone, which is a long bone that makes up part of the shoulder girdle. It rotates along its axis and keeps the arm away from the thorax so the arm has maximum range of movement.

CLAVICULAR BREATHING
Breathing that is characterized by heaving the chest up and down so the shoulders are engaged by rising during inhalation. This is very inefficient breath for singing.

COSTAL MUSCLES
The muscles woven in and around the rib cage. There are two sets: the internal-intercostal muscles and the external-intercostal muscles. The external-intercostals help lift and separate the rib cage during inhalation and the internal-intercostals move the ribs inward and slightly downward during exhalation.

A knowledge
of terms and
definitions
will facilitate
learning when
reading about
singing.

Additional Terms

Research Notes

DIAPHRAGM
A double-dome shaped tendonous muscle lying horizontally in the body separating the thorax from the abdominal cavity. This muscle acts as a pump which flattens for inhalation, displacing the viscera (or internal organs of the body), causing exhalation. Simultaneously, the rib cage opens (by action of the intercostal muscles) and lifts slightly during inhalation creating a partial vacuum in the thorax which causes the lungs to fill with air. Exhalation is a reverse action of this activity of the ribs, muscles, and diaphragm which allows air to leave the lungs.

EPIGLOTTIS
The cartilage that closes over the trachea during swallowing to protect the lungs from food or water.

EPIGASTRIUM
Literally "covering of the stomach" which is the upper part of the abdominal wall above the umbilicus (belly button), or the upper third of the frontal abdominal wall. It is the highest median region of the abdomen and can be felt as an inverted "v" between the costal regions jut below the sternum.

ESOPHAGUS
A muscular tube which carries food from the pharynx to the stomach. The esophagus lies directly behind the trachea.

FACH
A method of classifying singers (primarily opera singers), by range, weight, and color of their voices. Many opera roles are classified as a specific *fach* and professional singers may be hired based on their specific vocal category. An excellent source for research is *Singers' Edition: Operatic Arias* by Robert Boldrey and Janet Bookspan with various contributing authors.

FOCUS
Sometimes called the clarity and vibrancy of the tone. It is the concentration and intensity of sound that is balanced in color and dynamics with the presence of overtones. The sound is not produced too darkly nor too brightly.

Understanding
concepts
begins with
understanding
terms and
definitions.

Additional Terms

Research Notes

FORMANTS
Regions of high spectral energy resulting in resonant peaks of the voice are called vocal formants.

GLOTTIS
The space, between the vocal cords: the glottis is open during breathing and closes during swallowing and phonation.

HARD PALATE
The hard surfaced roof of the mouth found directly behind the front teeth extending midway in the roof of the mouth. This area is important for articulation and reverberation of the tone.

HEAD VOICE
The upper part of the voice where perceived sensation (created by sympathetic vibration) is often described as "in the head". All singers have a head register which should be developed for a freely produced vocal line throughout the range.

HYOID BONE
The U-shaped bone at the top portion of the larynx. The tongue is attached to the hyoid bone and the thyroid cartilage is suspended from it.

HYPOGASTRIUM
The abdominal wall below the umbilicus (belly button).

IMAGERY
The use of images or thoughts not specifically related to singing which gives concepts of space, line, energy or movement to the singer. For instance, to make more space in the mouth and throat the teacher might ask the student to imagine that there is a space in the throat large enough for an orange.

INTENSITY
Usually thought of in terms of brilliance, energy or core of the tone. There are different characteristics that combine to make an exciting concentration of sound, but none of them require pushing or driving the voice.

Artists allow music to come to life within the context of pitch, rhythm, style and expression.

Additional Terms

Research Notes

LARYNX
Commonly known as the voice box. The muscles and cartilage surrounding the vocal cords are housed in the larynx where tone it produced.

LEGATO
A smooth, connected vocal line - singing with an even tone through the phrase with no obvious or heavy adjustments between notes.

MELISMA
Commonly known as a vocal run, it is the technique of singing a single syllable of text while rapidly changing pitches. This technique has been used for centuries in all styles of vocal music.

MUCOSA
The soft tissues of the larynx, particularly the vocal folds, which is key to vibration of the cords during phonation.

MUSICALITY
Musicality is the art of interpretation and understanding of songs and arias sung with artistic and sensitive styling. Artists allow music to come to life within the context of pitch, rhythm, style and expression.

OPTIMUM PITCH
The area of the voice best suited for speaking. Those who habitually speak too high or too low will notice vocal strain and sometimes chronic hoarseness. Continual strain on the voice can result in vocal nodules; therefore, if there is a possibility that you might be speaking out of range, ask your voice teacher to test your speaking voice for optimum pitch.

OVERTONES
The harmonics of the sung pitch. Every tone we sing has additional pitches within the initial sound. When the primary note is sung (the fundamental pitch), there are also a series of other pitches aboove it called the "overtones". The first overtone is an octave above the fundamental pitch, the second is an octave and a fifth above the fundamental pitch, the third overtone is two octaves above and so on. The presence of overtones determines the tone color of the pitch. Pressing or pushing the voice will shorten the overtone series and inhibit the natural and inherent beauty of the tone.

A primary
goal for
singers is to
find a balance
of tone that is
not too bright
nor too dark…

Additional Terms

Research Notes

PASSAGGIO
A grouping of transitional notes that fall between and connect registers. Some people refer to this area of the voice as transition notes, the bridge, or the lift.

PHARYNX
The throat. The pharynx extends from the top of the larynx to the back of the mouth and nasal passage.

PHRENIC NERVE
The phrenic nerve leads from the 3rd, 4th and 5th cervical spinal nerves (C3-C5) to the diaphragm. It controls contractions of the diaphragm which is necessary for inhalation and exhalation.

PROJECTION
How the voice "carries" in the room. This is NOT only related to volume. A focused, well-balanced tone sung softly (with the presence of overtones), will project even better than a tone that is pushed or over-sung.

PURE VOWELS
Vowels without influence or combination of differing sounds are considered to be pure. Many people refer to the Italian vowels as pure vowels; however, any vowel can be purely produced if there is no other sound attached to the initial vowel.

REGISTER
An area of the voice with similarly produced tones and consistent timbre. There are four or five different areas of the voice experienced by singers and many differing opinions on how to define these areas. In *The Structure of Singing,* Dr. Richard Miller defines registers as Chest Voice, Mixed Voice, Head Voice, and Falsetto for men. For women, Chest Voice, Lower and Upper Middle, Head Voice and Flageolet. In *The Diagnosis and Correction of Vocal Faults,* Dr. James McKinney describes the normal phonational register as Modal Voice with three auxiliary registers being Vocal Fry, Falsetto, and Whistle.

A goal for singers is to connect the voice through the entire singing range without noticeable shifts.

Additional Terms

Research Notes

NOTE: The study of registers is quite interesting and sometimes controversial. Studying vocal registers will be an important topic not only in the studio, but also in Vocal Pedagogy, Master Classes and Vocal Seminars. No matter what nomenclature is used, the goal for singers is to connect the voice through the entire singing range without noticeable shifts.

RELEASING TENSION

There are many ways of counteracting the negative effects of too much tension in the body. First is recognizing problematic areas of tension. Next is to consciously release the muscles by relaxation and/or exercise (a good tool to use is a mirror).

A recurring problem for most singers is the tendency to tighten the jaw. One way to check if the jaw is dropping is to place the fingers directly in front of the ears while singing an open vowel. The hinge of the jaw opens, creating a space, when the jaw drops and relaxes. Many times tension in the shoulders can be relieved by gently rolling them forward and backward in a circular motion, then dropping them back and down.

RESONANCE

Re-sounding a tone. Increasing amplitude of an initial vibrating tone (the fundamental pitch), which intensifies and prolongs the sound. A number of different frequencies are present in the fundamental pitch, these tones enhance the initial sound through the overtone series. Pitch changes occur as resonant space is altered by the articulators.

RESONATORS

The vocal tract is made up of the throat (pharynx), the oral cavity, and nasal cavities. As air moves from the trachea into the larynx; tone is created by the vibration of the vocal cords coming together; the air then continues to move the tone from the larynx into the open cavities where sympathetic vibrating surfaces set up reverberation. This amplifies the vibrating tone. Changes in the vocal tract will color the sound and alter resonance.

SOFT PALATE

The soft tissue area of the roof of the mouth extending from mid-point back to the uvula. This area is important in helping increase or decrease space in the mouth as well as assisting in articulation and reverberation of the tone.

Resonance is increasing amplitude of an initial vibrating tone which intensifies and prolongs the sound.

Additional Terms

Research Notes

STERNUM

A long flat bone commonly known as the breast bone, the sternum is located in the center of the thorax and connects with the ribs to form a cage which helps protect the lungs and heart.

SUPPORT

Breath support for singers should actually be thought of as breath control or breath management. The goal is to have a secure foundation of breath for the tone without "squeezing in" the abdominal muscles or "forcing" the abdominal wall to become too tight and rigid. There is a delicate balance in not allowing exhalation to occur too rapidly without "locking" the breath. This balance of muscular activity is critical to correct control of the breath and should never be forced to either push out with strain or squeezed in with excessive tension. Support for singing is the even flow of breath without undue stress or tension – slowing the release of air by maintaining space in the ribs and thorax during singing.

TENSION

Tension in the body is completely necessary; otherwise, we would not be able to stand erect. Therefore, there is some "good tension" which all of us need for most activities. However, there is a culprit lurking in all of us which creates a destructive kind of tension. Constricting the muscles in any area of the body will affect singing adversely. We often see "bad" tension in the jaw, throat, mouth, neck, forehead, shoulders and arms in singers. Sometimes we even see too much tension in posture and the muscles related to breathing.

Tension can be alleviated through relaxation and stretching techniques to bring the body into balance for consistent and more efficient work. Ridding the body of unnecessary tension takes time and patience. Rely on your teacher to guide you to find balance in the body.

TESSITURA

Tessitura refers to the *pitch range that most frequently occurs* within a particular piece of music. Even though the range (lowest note to the highest note) of a song may be quite extensive, most of the pitches will fall into a shorter span of notes and this is the tessitura of the piece.

Constricting
the muscles
in any area
of the body
will adversely
affect singing.

Additional Terms

Research Notes

TRACHEA
The tube commonly known as the windpipe that extends from the larynx to the primary bronchi, allowing breath (air) to pass into the lungs. The larynx is positioned at the top of the trachea.

UVULA
The posterior, fleshy, conical point of the soft palate. It suspends from the soft palate as if it might be dropping into the throat.

VAGUS NERVE
The vagus nerve is the only nerve that starts in the brainstem and extends all the way to the abdomen. It is responsible for such varied tasks as heart rate, sweating, speech and keeping the larynx open for speaking and singing.

VIBRATO
The pitch variation that naturally occurs from normal vibration of the vocal cords. As the tone is sung, the vibrations set up ocillation of pitch above and below the fundamental tone; this variation adds warmth and beauty to the sound.

VOCAL CORDS
Vocal cords are ligaments housed within the larynx, which sits above the trachea and just below the thyroid cartilage. They are attached at the back (closest to the spinal cord) to the arytenoid cartilage and at the front (closest to the chin) to the thyroid cartilage. As air from the trachea passes through the larynx, vibration occurs between the vocal cords and this produces the initial sound. Vocal cords are the primary vibratory component of the voice box (larynx).

VOCAL FOLDS
Another name for vocal cords.

VOCAL LINE
This term refers to the way musical phrases are sung by individuals. Many times teachers or adjudicators will speak of a need to connect, emphasize, or enhance the vocal line. Usually, the preference is to sing expressively with a balance of energy, support, intensity and clarity.

It is
important for
singers
to learn
vowel
modification
in order
to maintain
a smooth,
uninterrupted
tone
throughout
the range.

Additional Terms

Research Notes

VOCAL NODULES

Callus-type hardening of the membrane on the vocal folds causing breathiness, a harsh or strident sound, and physical discomfort when singing. This vocal damage can be caused by singing and/or speaking out of range, improper vocal technique, or misusing the voice. Symptoms of illnesses or allergies resulting in chronic coughing or nasal drainage can also contribute to damaging the vocal cords. In most cases, vocal nodules (nodes), can be treated successfully. See a throat specialist immediately if you think you might have vocal nodules.

VOCAL ONSET

The initiation of tone when the air flow begins over adducted (closed) vocal cords and the vocal tract is set for singing.

VOCAL RANGE

The span from the highest to the lowest singable notes a particular voice can produce within a song.

VOCALIS MUSCLE

The primary body of the vocal fold is known as the vocalis muscle. It alters vocal fold tension and relaxation during speaking and singing to create varying pitch.

VOCALISES

Exercises for the voice. Usually, vocalises are prescribed by the teacher to assist singers in developing skill or strengthening an area of the voice. Vocalises are also used to warm-up the voice before long periods of singing.

VOICE BOX

The larynx is commonly known as the voice box.

VOWEL SPACE

The space in the throat and mouth given to a particular vowel. Many times a singer will provide too much or (most frequently) not enough space for vowels to reach resonant peaks during singing. Altering the vowel during sustained singing will also affect pitch and color.

Musical direction from a choral director, vocal coach, or artistic director is more likely to be understood if you know basic terms and musical definitions.

Additional Terms

Research Notes

VOWEL MODIFICATION

Altering pure vowels to unify the voice and maximize the format through the vocial range and maintain the same color and quality of the vowel. It would be impossible to sing the exact same vowel from chest voice through mid-range into head voice without noticing a dramatic change in the vowel and tonal quality of the voice; in fact, it is almost impossible to sing a pure closed vowel sound in the upper voice. Therefore, it is important for singers to learn vowel modification in order to maintain a smooth, uninterrupted tone throughout the range.

Phonation

When air passes from the lungs into the trachea through the true vocal folds, vibration occurs. Depending on the length and density of the folds, this vibration produces different pitches. The resonating chambers and articulators literally shape the sound and color the tone. The false vocal folds, which sit above the true vocal folds are not responsible for creating a tone; however, they do vibrate because of the movement of air through the ventricle of Morgagni and the proximity to the true vocal folds.

The following three pages are labeled diagrams of the head, torso, and larynx. By familiarizing yourself with the location of muscles, cartilage, and organs, you can better understand the process of singing.

Learning the physiological make-up of the body gives the singer a clearer mental image of the vocal tract, which will assist in understanding how the vocal instrument works.

Resonators are found...

Tone is produced by...

Brightness/Darkness is determined by...

To allow more space for resonance one must...

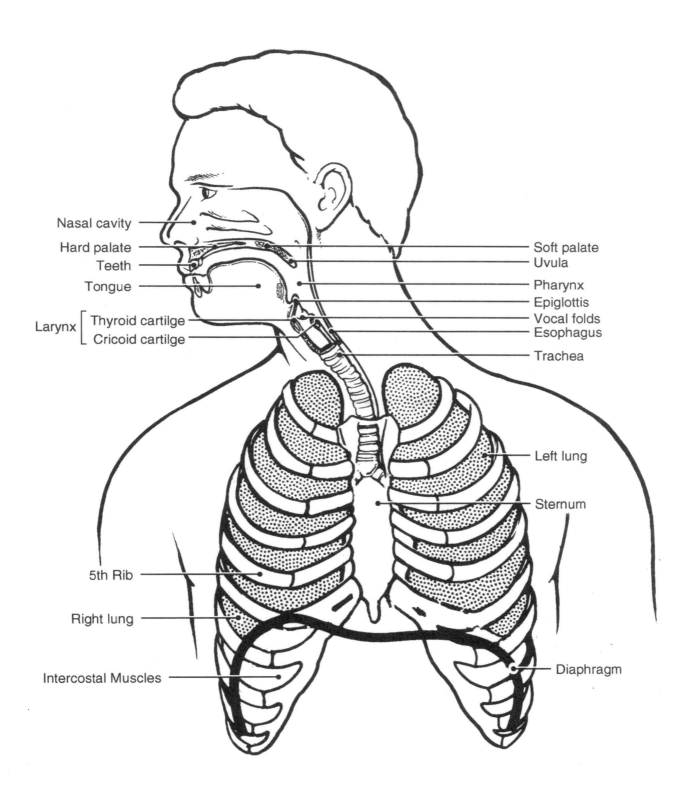

Nasal cavity

Hard palate

Teeth

Tongue

Larynx [Thyroid cartilge
         Cricoid cartilge

Soft palate

Uvula

Pharynx

Epiglottis

Vocal folds

Esophagus

Trachea

Left lung

Sternum

5th Rib

Right lung

Intercostal Muscles

Diaphragm

Physiology of the Vocal Instrument

Fill In The Blank

Need help? Review Terms and Definitions beginning on page 23.

1. The leaf-shaped cartilage that tilts back over the trachea during swallowing (to protect the lungs), is the _____.

2. The protective cartilage at the front and sides of the larynx is the _____.

3. The folds at the top of the trachea that vibrate to create sounds are the _____.

4. The tube responsible for moving food from the pharynx into the stomach is the _____.

5. Name the articulators _____.

6. Another name for the voice box is the _____.

7. The tube extending from the pharynx to the primary bronchi is called the _____.

LARYNX
(FRONTAL SECTION)

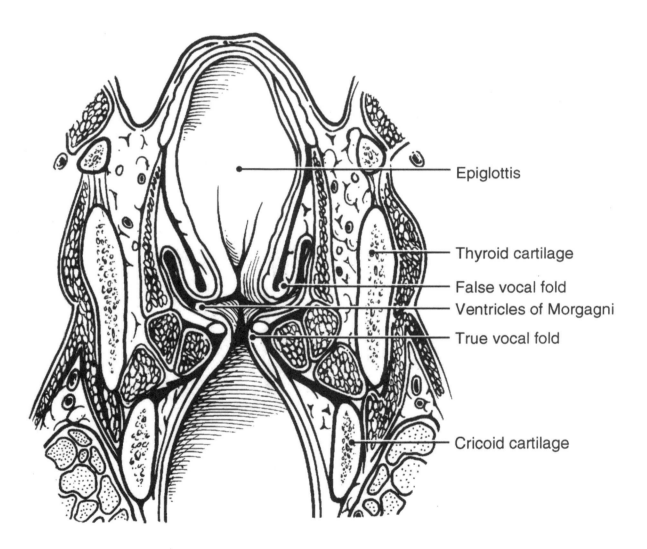

Epiglottis

Thyroid cartilage

False vocal fold

Ventricles of Morgagni

True vocal fold

Cricoid cartilage

Pop
Quiz

Why is it important to understand the physiological make-up of the body?

Can you describe the process of breathing for singing and name the muscles involved?

LARYNX

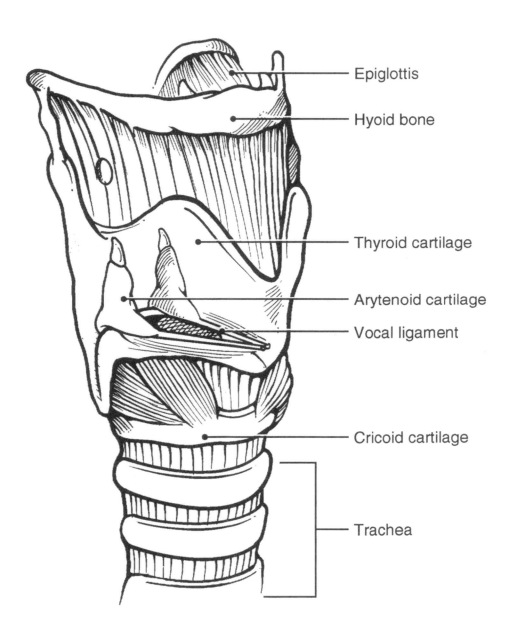

Epiglottis

Hyoid bone

Thyroid cartilage

Arytenoid cartilage

Vocal ligament

Cricoid cartilage

Trachea

To gain maximum benefit from practice sessions, you must be organized and goal oriented. Knowing what you want to accomplish in daily practice sessions will result in productive practice. Methodical practice will give you a sense of accomplishment which results in a positive self-image and an enthusiastic attitude about singing.

HOW TO PRACTICE

*The importance of practice cannot be over-emphasized!
Developing your talent is up to you; therefore, consistent and
methodical practice on a daily basis should be your personal goal.*

Make a complete weekly schedule on the forms found in this book. Include every daily activity – do not leave anything out. Keep one copy and give the other to your teacher.

Set aside 1-2 hours every day for practice – if you absolutely need one day free, that is fine. It will be best for you to practice two shorter periods each day rather than one long session. Guard this time carefully!!! It is the only opportunity that you have to solidify what you have learned in the studio. Without **daily** practice, you are not **building** and **developing** your voice to reach its full potential.

Commit to scheduling practice time every day. Practice for the full length of time scheduled without interruptions from others! Make this time each week a top priority!!

Go into the practice room every day with a good attitude! Approach your practice positively and enthusiastically. Use the scheduled time only for practicing voice and try to leave problems outside the door.

Steps For Successful Practice

1 Begin by aligning the body correctly. Correct posture is the only way correct breath can be achieved. Refer to the guide on posture if you need help.

2 Next, do breathing exercises. Concentrate on the importance of breath and how your muscles react to each exercise. Note sensations during the exercise, especially if you feel tension. Relieve tension immediately so you can continue to build on a balanced muscular system. Remember that **the breath is the foundation for the tone**; therefore, these exercises deserve your full attention!

Probably the most difficult step toward effective practice is actually walking into the practice room. That is why committing to a schedule is so important. Learning to say 'no" to external distractions and staying on track is critical to consistent practice.

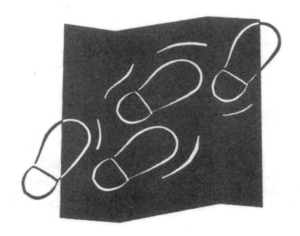

Practice does not make a perfect performance; Perfect practice makes a perfect performance.

3 After posture and breathing have been established, begin vocalizing. Begin with very simple exercises from mid-range to the top voice and back down to the lowest note in your range, then back to mid-range. After the voice feels awake and free, and vowel sounds are consistent through the range, you may move into more difficult exercises or those that challenge you. NEVER force your voice to sing out of range! Your teacher will assign exercises to increase your range, but again, there is a delicate balance that must be respected in these exercises.

4 Attention to the voice during vocal exercises is extremely important. Listen to yourself. What is your voice doing? How do you sound? Is the tone freely produced or does it sound tense, strained or strident? Do you hear an "honest" sound or are you over-producing and working too hard? How does your throat feel? Do you feel freedom in the throat or is the tongue creating tension, or are muscles tightening in the throat? Is your jaw relaxed open or is it clenched? Is your vibrato consistent or do you hear straight tones in these exercises? Are you able to sing with contrasting dynamics? Are you getting the same tonal production you had in your lesson? These are a few of the questions you should be asking yourself during practice. Concentration is essential as you listen to your voice. A well-trained ear will be your greatest friend.

5 Next, begin work on literature. Start with a familiar song or one you are excited about learning. Again, take your time. Look at the poetry or prose. Who is the composer? When was the song written? Is it from a larger work? Do you understand the text? Do you know who you are portraying in this song or aria? Why are you singing this song? If it is a foreign language, do you know the pronunciation? What are you trying to convey in this song or aria? Answer these questions before you begin to sing. Singing is an art form that requires total involvement from the artist. Give attention to every detail of every phrase. Follow the same ideas of listening to your voice as you did in the vocalises.

Keep your music organized and together in a binder.

Give copies of your music to your accompanist.

Learn your music before meeting with your accompanist to maximize rehearsal time.

Keep a table of contents for your binder for quick reference.

Stay focused in the rehearsal time with your accompanist so your session is productive.

Get to the appointed earsal time early enough to stretch the body.

Organize and direct the rehearsal session with your accompanist to get more accomplished.

Keep a blank cassette tape or CD in your music folder to record lessons and/or practice sessions.

> **Do not fall into the pattern of mindlessly singing through your literature.**

6 After you have thoroughly practiced the first song, begin working on another that is more difficult. You may need to work on particular sections of songs or arias that seem to be problematic. However, try to incorporate that section into the entire phrase before ending your practice so you will not always see that section as a barrier.

7 If time permits, go to another song. If you find that you are getting tired, stop singing for a while. You can use short breaks to work on pronunciation, translation of languages, rhythms, inflection, enunciation, characterization, and communication of the text. NOTE: If you are singing a foreign language art song or aria, it is extremely important to translate the text before you learn the music. Singing without understanding the meaning of the song inhibits every aspect of learning and performing.

8 As part of your regularly scheduled practice sessions, go to the music library and listen to great artists singing the songs and arias that you are singing. Hearing professional singers on a consistent basis helps develop your sense of musicality and artistry.

> **The way you practice is the way you will sing.**

Work on memorizing your literature as soon as possible. If you can move away from the music, you can concentrate more on tonal production, pronunciation, technique and interpretation. It should be easy for you to memorize one or more songs per week if you are spending an adequate number of hours in the practice room. Exceptions to this expectation are rare.

Sight reading involves three components:

1. **Rhythm**

2. **Melody**

3. **Words**

Work on each of these separately so you are not overwhelmed by the task.

Sight reading is an important skill to learn – sight ready every day!

Another challenge that you should take for yourself is sight-reading melodies. Use about three minutes of each practice session to sing through phrases of unfamiliar songs. Sight-reading has two benefits: first, you will learn more literature, and the second is that you will increase your ability to sight-read, which will serve you well in the future.

Sight-reading is easy; simply find a song that you do not know. Look at the first four measures, establish the key in which the song is written, and first tap out the rhythm (even if it is an easy rhythm, do this as an exercise). Next try to sing the melody on one vowel without getting help from playing the melody on the piano. Now you are ready to read the four measures again with words. After you have sung those four measures, check yourself on the piano and correct any mistakes. Then repeat the process on the next four measures. Doing this exercise for only a few minutes during each practice session will be fun and it will enhance your sight-reading ability almost immediately.

Before leaving the practice room, make a few quick notes about your session on the practice schedule sheet. This will assist you in organizing your practice times and it will give you an overall view of what you have accomplished. Keeping records is a good way to monitor your personal progress.

Do not sing when you are experiencing hoarseness, edema, or laryngitis. Your body is telling you to slow down.

WHAT TO DO IF YOU ARE SICK

When you are sick, determine whether you have an infection, a common cold, or allergies. If you have an infection, go to the doctor and begin taking prescribed medication. Please do not prolong a serious illness by trying to wait it out.

If you have allergies, you may already have an effective medication to help you through the allergy seasons. If not, and your condition is detrimental to your singing, please see a health care professional who may refer you to an allergy specialist. Please do not subject yourself to unnecessary illness, especially if your condition can be treated.

If your vocal cords are swollen or if you have laryngitis (if you have lost your voice), it will be better not to sing for a few days until the swelling disappears. It is much better to miss a few days of singing than to push your voice to sing on swollen vocal cords.

If you have a common cold or you are feeling somewhat hoarse, there are some positive things that you can do to help relieve the symptoms.

➤ Get plenty of sleep. Do not stay up late – you need the rest!

➤ Drink a lot of water. It will hydrate the body and will help keep the mucous membranes from drying out so quickly. Flooding your system with water will help your body regain the balance necessary to fight the common cold, allergies and infections. Do not drink coffee, tea or carbonated drinks for hydration during illness.

➤ If your system will tolerate this medication, take two ibuprofen every 4-6 hours for two or three days. This will help reduce swelling in the cords.

➤ Stop talking. Using your voice to speak or whisper can cause stress and strain on the larynx. Your hoarse voice needs some quiet time to return to normal.

➤ Use a saline solution nasal spray. This is a good way to hydrate the nasal passages which will again help the mucous membranes stay balanced.

Take A Minute

When you are on a busy schedule, try short relaxation exercises to refresh your body and mind.

1. Sit or stand tall with your weight evenly distributed.

2. Inhale and exhale slowly – repeating four times.

3. Roll shoulders in complete circles backward and forward.

4. Shake your hands freely for four seconds to relieve tension.

5. Burrrr the lips (raspberry), then in an extremely exaggerated fashion, silently and slowly mouth the work "yikes" to relax the facial muscles.

➤ DO NOT TAKE ANTIHISTAMINES. This medication will dry out the entire vocal tract which will create more problems for you. Antihistamines actually cause secretions in the nose, throat, and lungs to thicken which can contribute to bronchial and sinus infections. If you need medication to help relieve pressure in the sinuses, take a decongestant. Of course, there are some people who need to take antihistamines. If your doctor prescribes this medication, discuss the side effects with him/her and let your doctor know that you are a singer.

➤ It is fine to help keep the mouth moist with gum or plain mints; however, menthol can act as a drying agent working against the delicate membranes of the vocal tract.

➤ Stand in a warm shower a little longer than usual; use a cool mist vaporizer, or run hot water in the sink and place a towel over your head while you breathe in the steam. All of these are suggestions to help guard against the drying agents of the air we breathe, especially dry heat in our homes, apartments, or dormitories.

➤ Eat a balanced diet. When you are ill, protein in the body is used more rapidly – requiring more attention to proper diet. Fuel the body correctly and it will work more efficiently, especially if energy is required to fight illness.

➤ Wash your hands frequently to guard against spreading germs to others. Be considerate of those around you when you are ill.

➤ It is fine to drink warm liquids to soothe the throat, but please do not think that this will directly affect the vocal cords. Liquids no not pass through the vocal cords (the epiglottis protects the trachea and larynx from food and drink being swallowed). Because the liquid is warm, it will, however, warm the muscles close to the larynx. One note of caution: drink warm liquid instead of hot liquid. If the temperature is too hot, it can actually cause additional swelling in the throat.

➤ Some people advocate taking large doses of vitamin C to help them get over a cold. No conclusive evidence points to vitamin therapy as a remedy for illness; however, many individuals feel strongly that the benefits far outweigh any slight risks. If you feel better taking vitamins, then by all means do it!

> A recent hospital publication suggests that eating yogurt will help the body fight the common cold.

Many people use caffeine products (colas, coffee, tea, chocolate, and some medications), to start the day or as a periodic "pick me up". Normally, these products do not create serious health problems and caffeine may even be prescribed to treat some health problems. However, sensitivity to caffeine can surface quickly. The following symptoms are common indicators of caffeine sensitivity.

Headaches
Nervousness
Dryness in the throat
Blurred vision
Weight gain
Heart palpitations

Caffeine withdrawal can also cause some of these same symptoms; therefore, gradual reduction of caffeine will help to minimize the effects of withdrawal.

See your doctor if you experience any of these symptoms. Caffeine sensitivity is easily treated, but these symptoms can also indicate other more complicated health problems.

MAINTAINING A HEALTHY VOICE

Your voice is a unique and beautiful instrument. Unlike any other instrument ever created, your voice has incomparable qualities that represent you as an individual. Your voice communicates to the rest of the world your ideas, your emotions, and your art. The human voice stands alone among all musical instruments because of the unparalleled colors, expressions, and qualities it is capable of producing. Your voice, the human instrument, can convey to the listener images and texts as well as musical phrases. The voice is not an inanimate object; it is vibrant and alive.

The human voice is also different from other instruments because you never leave it. Your voice is with you twenty-four hours a day. It is part of your body; therefore, everything that you do affects this beautiful instrument! If you are physically or emotionally tired, it shows in your voice. If you are upset or angry, it is expressed through your voice. If you are ill, it affects every part of your vocal tract. Therefore, it is important for you as a singer to take positive steps in maintaining your voice.

❖ **Eat a balanced diet.** The body must have nutrients to work efficiently which means that the voice requires the same dietary nutrients.

❖ **Get plenty of sleep and rest daily.** The body (and voice) must have rest to sustain life. If you continually deplete the body of necessary sleep, your well-being will be seriously affected.

❖ **Drink plenty of water!** Your body is largely water and you must replenish the reservoir regularly to maintain a healthy balance in muscles and tissue to keep you going! Water is just as important as food in fueling the body and the voice.

❖ **Use medication sparingly** – especially any drug that dries out the mucous membranes. Remember, everything that affects your body also affects your voice. Introducing chemicals into the body can affect both adversely.

❖ **Watch caffeine intake.** Too much caffeine can cause health problems which directly affect the voice. Why not opt for water most of the time?

❖ **Smoking.** There is nothing positive and there is so much negative that can be said for smoking or using tobacco products. Don't do it!

Getting into a regular routine of exercise will make you feel better immediately. Start slowly at first then work up to longer periods of exercise each week. If you don't like the thought of an exercise class or workout video, try walking. Any exercise that utilizes the large muscles will energize the body by increasing circulation. If exercising represents a major life change for you – check with your doctor before beginning an exercise regimen.

Hints and Reminders

During exercise:

➤ Guard against locking the breath while lifting weights because it causes laryngeal pressure.

➤ Cover the mouth and nose loosely in winter while working or exercising outside.

➤ Remember to breathe deeply during exercise and running rather than shallow clavicular breathing.

➤ Schedule exercise time into your weekly schedule sheet.

➤ **Alcohol and Drugs.** Any type of mind-altering drug can become problematic within weeks of initial use, and usually there is no warning that the user can become dependent on the drug. Let me encourage you to think seriously about the psychological and physiological effects that recreational drugs and alcohol have on your body. The time to make decisions about drug use is now, before the question comes up.

➤ **Exercise regularly.** Nothing energizes the body like aerobic exercise. It helps the muscles stay toned, it improves circulation, and it helps the mind stay focused, which means that the entire body runs more efficiently. Exercise will assist in overall conditioning of the body, mind, and spirit.

➤ **Wash your hands frequently.** This sounds like your mother talking, but it is great advice. Singers are a gregarious group which means that we are with other people almost constantly. We shake hands or hug other people often and we are bombarded with airborne germs and germs from inanimate objects continually. The average person touches their face (nose, mouth or eyes) about three times per hour, so it is easy to see how quickly germs enter our body every day! Assist your immune system by being pro-active in germ warfare.

➤ **Practice.** The importance of consistent practice cannot be emphasized too much. This is the opportunity you have to build sound vocal technique, thereby securing a strong foundation for developing the voice. It is the best way to put into practice what you have accomplished in your private lessons and it provides ample opportunity to learn and memorize literature. Practice time can be the most productive time of your week. Schedule practice every day as though it were a class. Guard these hours and don't let anything keep you from practicing. You will be amazed at the progress you see after only a few weeks.

Take care of yourself. Use common sense about your overall health. Your voice is part of your body; therefore, it is affected by everything you do.

Music of all styles and cultures can be performed with correct vocal technique. Remember the basics of good singing and never sing out of your range; sing too loudly; or abuse the voice by manufacturing or pressing the sound.

- **Speak at optimum pitch.** There is an area of your voice which is best suited for habitual speech – speaking above or below it will produce laryngeal pressure which can eventually damage the vocal cords. Avoid unnecessary damage by speaking in the "comfort zone." Your voice teacher can help locate your optimum pitch.

- **Avoid extremes in speech.** This means no yelling (try to restrain yourself at concerts and ball games!), no strained speech, no whispering or whinny speaking and do not speak out of your range. All of these can cause vocal problems.

- **Sing comfortably within your range,** using good vocal technique. Pressurized singing or unsupported singing and singing either too low or too high will cause vocal problems.

- Possibly the most important component in maintaining a healthy voice is to **think positively!** Having a positive outlook on life affects your attitude about everything you do – including studying and practicing. When you feel better, you have more energy and it is easier to accomplish daily tasks. You seem to have more time in the day because you use time more efficiently. Your self image is more positive; therefore, you interact more confidently with others. A positive approach in voice lessons means that you will learn and retain more quickly, so you come away having achieved more during the lesson. The benefits of a positive attitude are immediate, and it certainly has an effect on your future as well.

Vocalizing using a piano is preferred because of flexibility in meeting your specific goals; however, you don't have to be a concert pianist to play the vocalizes. If you know the pattern of the vocalize (examples are found in the next section), simply begin by striking one note on the piano and move up or down by half steps as you complete each vocalise. Remember to stay within your vocal range and NEVER strain or push the voice.

The emphasis is on listening carefully to the voice, not on how well you play the piano. Listen for: tonal production, vowel migration, flexibility, breath management and other technical aspects of singing. Some singers practice in rooms where a piano is not available; others even like to vocalize while driving (only if you have both hands on the steering wheel and you remain alert to traffic conditions). The accompanying CD is useful for those times when you are not able to use a piano during vocal exercises.

Vocalises

Exercises for the Voice

Guide to Vocalises

Proper posture and breathing technique is fundamental in preparing for vocalization. Use a mirror to check your posture and refer to the section on Breathing for Singing for guidance in breath management.

Vowels for each exercise have been suggested; however, using different vowels on all of the exercises will be beneficial to you as you learn to sing consistently through the range.

Exercise 1 Humming is an easy way to wake-up the voice. Separate the teeth and concentrate the buzz in the front of the mouth (at times, you may feel that the lips are vibrating).

Exercise 2 This three-note exercise is another very good way to start warming-up the voice. Sing smoothly and evenly, letting the tone travel forward in the mouth.

Exercise 3 Connect the "zing" through to the "ah" without adjusting the tone; then allow the 16th notes to stay forward rather than dropping as you continue singing with equal energy to the end of the phrase.

Exercise 4 Singing a legato line while changing vowels is sometimes difficult. Listen for consistently open, pure vowels even through the sustained vowel sound.

Exercise 5 This arpeggio should feel free and easy to the voice. Try to keep the sound moving forward rather than "reaching" for the top note.

Exercise 6 Sing each note clearly and separately in a light, freely produced approach. Use other vowels in this exercise as you increase flexibility.

Exercise 7 Keep this staccato exercise energized throughout the phrase as you sing each note with equal pressure.

Exercise 8 Sing this interval of a 5th with a smooth vocal line as one vowel sound develops into another. Try to sing without added weight in the voice.

If You Vocalize While Driving

Make the most effective use of the practice CD in the car by...

→ Being aware of posture when driving.

→ Staying alert at the wheel!

→ Following the recorded accompaniment.

→ Being aware of full expansion of the breath.

→ Staying within your range and concentrating on breathing if the accompaniment moves beyond your range.

Exercise 9   This agility exercise should be sung as freely as possible to articulate each note clearly while maintaining a connected line.

Exercise 10   The combination exercise of an octave leap, sustained singing and agility development requires concentration on all three techniques. Sing this exercise with a fluid line.

Exercise 11   Singing triplets is another kind of flexibility exercise. Use the plosive sound of the consonant to move from one vowel to another, articulating each note of the vocalise.

Exercise 12   Sing this exercise slowly and listen to the smooth connection between notes. The dynamic changes should reflect consistent vocal control without creating tension.

Exercise 13   This vocalise is a good tone initiation exercise. Actually take a breath every time it is marked and move into the next tone with equalized breath pressure and tone. Try to eliminate harsh vocal adjustments during vocal re-entry.

Exercise 14   Sing this exercise evenly without "shifting" the tone to accommodate the octave. Try to think of these notes on one plane.

Exercise 15   This sequence of thirds offers a challenge to sing the progression evenly while maintaining correct tuning. Watch the tendency to use aspirates as you sing the third.

Exercise 16   The descending five note scale can be very relaxing to the voice. Singing the "yah" on each note can also assist you in loosening the jaw. Also, try different combinations of consonants and vowels on this exercise.

Exercise 17   The object of this exercise is to connect each note into a continuous sound. The pitches will change, but the vocal line should remain fluid.

Exercise 18   Another combination melisma-staccato exercise which works line, energy, vibrancy and articulation of the tone.

Watch Yourself In A Mirror

As you begin your practice session, stand n front of a full-length mirror. By watching yourself, you will become aware of subtleties in muscular movement which affect posture, breathing, vocalizing and singing.

Exercise 19 This sequence of descending melismas combined with an octave run requires facile articulation of the tone and a developed sense of legato technique. Make sure that the tone color remains constant.

Exercise 20 An opportunity to practice breath management is found in this repetitive staccato exercise combined with the connected fifth. Sustain the breath by allowing the ribs and the abdominal wall to remain open as long as possible so the muscles are not forced in too quickly.

Exercise 21 This is a mirror vocalise to Exercise 19, which means that the sequence is ascending. Again, listen for the connected tone, free from tonal alteration.

Exercise 22 Another combination exercise which gives an opportunity for breath management, tonal balance, legato technique and staccato singing. Maintain energy and vibrancy throughout the exercise.

Exercise 23 A favorite melismatic exercise encompassing the 9th emphasizes line, fluidity, and tonal articulation. Try this exercise with all vowel sounds.

Record Your Progress

Kinesthetic Learning

During practice, if you have difficulty in particular areas, do not be afraid to involve the body to assist in relaxing the mind. Movement opens the body and energizes the mind; therefore, creating another way to establish the connection of mind and body in singing.

Try the following examples of kinesthetic learning:

☞ Move your arms in circles to assist in singing continuous or legato lines.

☞ Move your hand from your mouth straight forward to encourage the tone to come forward in the mouth.

☞ Hold arms in a large sphere overhead to envision more vowel space.

The following 23 vocalises are exercises for the voice. They are designed to assist you in developing skills and techniques essential for the singer. These exercises will reduce tension that causes fatigue and limitations to vocal development. Vocal control is important because it relates to the ability to...

- ◆ manage the breath for slow, sustained singing,
- ◆ maintain flexibility in the voice,
- ◆ sing uniform staccato phrases, and
- ◆ execute melismatic passages.

Initiating a tone with balanced breath, muscular activity, and acoustic space will produce a free, clear, and resonant sound. Observing how the voice works and setting realistic goals for becoming proficient in each exercise will assist you in a systematic approach to vocal development. In order to monitor progress effectively, try working on only three vocal exercises per week. Limiting the number of different exercises will help you concentrate on skill development.

Suggestion: After you have completed the practice sheet for the week, keep the original in this book for personal reference and make a copy the practice sheet for your teacher.

In order to monitor progress effectively, try working on only three different exercises per week.

Vocalises

(1) (Humming)

(2) zih   zih   zih zih zih
moh   moh   mohmohmoh

(3) zing - ah   zing-eh   zing - ee_____

4   mah - meh - mih - moh   moo

(5) lah   lah   lah   lah   lah lah lah

Vocalises

ah   ah   ah   ah   ah
ih   ih   ih   ih   ih

ih   ih   ih   ih   ih   ih   ih   ih   ih
ah   ah   ah   ah   ah   ah   ah   ah   ah

ee   oh   ee

zee

ah

Vocalises

11   deh— dah— deh— dah— doh

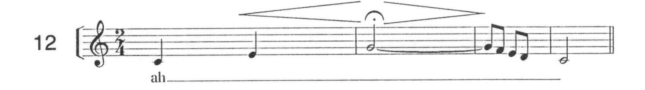

12   ah

13   ah   ah— ah— ah— ah—

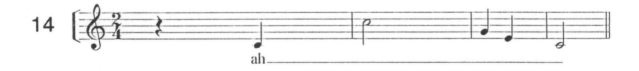

14   ah

15   mah— meh— mih— moh— moo

Vocalises

16   yah yah yah yah yah

17   ee

18   ee

19   ee

20   ih

<u>Vocalises</u>

21

ih
ah

22

ih
ah

23

ah

Additional Vocalises

Notes:

- don't focus on every little sound when singing. takes away from the sound and overall performance causing strain and keeps you from staying in time.

- Let loose, or "belt it out", don't keep it in and try to make your voice sound like something it's not.

Suggested Reading

Appelman, D. Ralph, *Science of Vocal Pedagogy*, Bloomington, Indiana: University Press, 1986.

Bunch, Meribeth, *Dynamics of the Singing Voice*, New York: Springer, 1997

Cameron, Julia with Mark Bryan, *The Artist's Way: A Spiritual Path to Higher Creativity*, New York, G.P. Putnam's Sons, 1992.

Doscher, Barbara, *The Functional Unity of the Singing Voice*; 2nd Ed., The Scarecrow Press, Inc.

McKinney, James C., *The Diagnosis and Correction of Vocal Faults*, Nashville, Tennessee: Broadman Press, 1982.

Miller, Richard, *The Structure of Singing, New York*: Schirmer Books, a division of Macmillan, Inc., 1986.

Radionoff, Sharon, *"Breath: The Fundamental Element of Singing"*, Texas Sings, Fall l994, 15-17.

Sataloff, Robert Thayer, *"Medications and Their Effects on the Voice"*, Journal of Singing, September/October 1995, 47-52.

Schmidt, Jan, *Basics of Singing*, New York: Schirmer Books, a division of Macmillan, Inc., l984.

Sheppard, David, *A Resource Guide for the Alexander Technique*, 1023 Menalto Ave., Menlo Park, CA 94025.

Wormhoudt, Pearl Shinn, *Building the Voice as an Instrument*, Oskaloosa, Iowa: William Penn College, l99l.

Additional source of articles for and about singers can be found in Journal of Singing, a publication of the National Association of Teachers of Singing and on the internet under various topics of singing and vocal pedagogy.

The quotes in the Practice Journal, unless otherwise stated, are from: *A Dictionary of Musical Quotations* by Ian Crofton and Donald Fraser, Schirmer Books, A Division of Macmillan, Inc., New York, 1985.

Weekly Schedule

TIME	MONDAY	TUESDAY	WEDNESDAY	THURSDAY	FRIDAY	SATURDAY	SUNDAY
8:00							
9:00							
10:00							
11:00							
12:00							
1:00							
2:00							
3:00							
4:00							
5:00							
6:00							
7:00							
8:00							
9:00							
10:00							

After completing your personal weekly schedule, make a copy for your teacher. This will help solidify your commitment to consistent daily practice.

Weekly Schedule

TIME	MONDAY	TUESDAY	WEDNESDAY	THURSDAY	FRIDAY	SATURDAY	SUNDAY
8:00	Still asleep (usually)						
9:00	Shower + get ready						
10:00	Finish getting ready +						
11:00	listening to the radio						
12:00							
1:00							
2:00							
3:00							
4:00							
5:00							
6:00							
7:00	eat + watch Pokemon						
8:00	reading/ laying on						
9:00	bed, trying to						
10:00	sleep						

WHEN PREPARING TO SING AN ARIA

Record on your practice sheet the ...

✍ story of the opera
✍ why the character is singing this aria
✍ significance of the period the opera was written
✍ composer data
✍ English translation
✍ information about the character

With any piece of music

It is important to know and record...

☞ the name of the composer
☞ the period it was written
☞ the translation, if written in a foreign language
☞ and if it is from a larger work, the significance
   of that piece within the work
☞ the style of the piece

Practice Journal

The following practice sheets are provided for you to record each practice session within a specific week. *Keeping a journal* is an effective way to observe patterns, recognize strengths and areas for growth, and chart personal progress. By keeping these practice sheets together, you will have a quick review of weekly practice. Using these practice sheets consistently will help you establish effective patterns for practicing.

Observations, Questions, Concerns, and Notes

No instrument
is satisfactory
except in so
far as it
approximates
to the sound
of the human
voice.

—Carl Maria
von Weber,
Letters, 1817

Posture:

Breathing:

Listening:

Sight-reading:

Information about songs / arias:

Songs memorized:

Practice Sheet

Date:	Date:	Date:	Date:
Vocalises	Vocalises	Vocalises	Vocalises
Katy Perry	Melanie Martinez		
Songs	Songs	Songs	Songs
Roar	D-o-l-l H-o-u-s-e		
Hours Practiced	Hours Practiced	Hours Practiced	Hours Practiced
30 minutes	1 hour — 30 min		

Date:	Date:	Date:	Lesson Day
Vocalises	Vocalises	Vocalises	Vocalises
Songs	Songs	Songs	
Hours Practiced	Hours Practiced	Hours Practiced	Total Hours Practiced

Music is said
to be the
speech of
angles.

—Carlyle,
*Essays The
Opera*

Observations, Questions, Concerns, and Notes

Posture:

Breathing:

Listening:

Sight-reading:

Information about songs / arias:

Songs memorized:

Practice Sheet

Date:	Date:	Date:	Date:
Vocalises	Vocalises	Vocalises	Vocalises
Songs	Songs	Songs	Songs
Hours Practiced	Hours Practiced	Hours Practiced	Hours Practiced

Date:	Date:	Date:	Lesson Day
Vocalises	Vocalises	Vocalises	Vocalises
Songs	Songs	Songs	
Hours Practiced	Hours Practiced	Hours Practiced	Total Hours Practiced

Observations, Questions, Concerns, and Notes

Music's the
medicine of
the mind.

—John Logan,
Danish Ode

Posture:

Breathing:

Listening:

Sight-reading:

Information about songs / arias:

Songs memorized:

Practice Sheet

Date:	Date:	Date:	Date:
Vocalises	Vocalises	Vocalises	Vocalises
Songs	Songs	Songs	Songs
Hours Practiced	Hours Practiced	Hours Practiced	Hours Practiced

Date:	Date:	Date:	Lesson Day
Vocalises	Vocalises	Vocalises	Vocalises
Songs	Songs	Songs	
Hours Practiced	Hours Practiced	Hours Practiced	Total Hours Practiced

Observations, Questions, Concerns, and Notes

Hasten slowly.

—Divus
Augustus

Posture:

Breathing:

Listening:

Sight-reading:

Information about songs / arias:

Songs memorized:

Practice Sheet

Practice Sheet

Date:	Date:	Date:	Date:
Vocalises	Vocalises	Vocalises	Vocalises
Songs	Songs	Songs	Songs
Hours Practiced	Hours Practiced	Hours Practiced	Hours Practiced

Date:	Date:	Date:	Lesson Day
Vocalises	Vocalises	Vocalises	Vocalises
Songs	Songs	Songs	
Hours Practiced	Hours Practiced	Hours Practiced	Total Hours Practiced

Observations, Questions, Concerns, and Notes

Sweetest the strain when in the song the singer has been lost.

—Elizabeth Stuart Phelps, *The Poet and the Poem.*

Posture:

Breathing:

Listening:

Sight-reading:

Information about songs / arias:

Songs memorized:

Practice Sheet

Date:	Date:	Date:	Date:
Vocalises	Vocalises	Vocalises	Vocalises
Songs	Songs	Songs	Songs
Hours Practiced	Hours Practiced	Hours Practiced	Hours Practiced
Date:	Date:	Date:	Lesson Day
Vocalises	Vocalises	Vocalises	Vocalises
Songs	Songs	Songs	
Hours Practiced	Hours Practiced	Hours Practiced	Total Hours Practiced

Observations, Questions, Concerns, and Notes

Alas, for those
that never
sing, but die
with all their
music in
them!

—O.W. Homes,
The Voiceless

Posture:

Breathing:

Listening:

Sight-reading:

Information about songs / arias:

Songs memorized:

Practice Sheet

Practice Sheet

Date:	Date:	Date:	Date:
Vocalises	Vocalises	Vocalises	Vocalises
Songs	Songs	Songs	Songs
Hours Practiced	Hours Practiced	Hours Practiced	Hours Practiced

Date:	Date:	Date:	Lesson Day
Vocalises	Vocalises	Vocalises	Vocalises
Songs	Songs	Songs	
Hours Practiced	Hours Practiced	Hours Practiced	Total Hours Practiced

Observations, Questions, Concerns, and Notes

Nothing great
was ever
achieved
without
enthusiasm.

—Ralph Waldo
Emerson

Posture:

Breathing:

Listening:

Sight-reading:

Information about songs / arias:

Songs memorized:

Practice Sheet

Date:	Date:	Date:	Date:
Vocalises	Vocalises	Vocalises	Vocalises
Songs	Songs	Songs	Songs
Hours Practiced	Hours Practiced	Hours Practiced	Hours Practiced

Date:	Date:	Date:	Lesson Day
Vocalises	Vocalises	Vocalises	Vocalises
Songs	Songs	Songs	
Hours Practiced	Hours Practiced	Hours Practiced	Total Hours Practiced

Observations, Questions, Concerns, and Notes

Music exalts
each joy,
allays each
grief,
expels
diseases,
soften every
pain, subdues
the rage of
poison, and
the plague.

—John
Armstrong, *Art
of Preserving
Health.*

Posture:

Breathing:

Listening:

Sight-reading:

Information about songs / arias:

Songs memorized:

Practice Sheet

Date:	Date:	Date:	Date:
Vocalises	Vocalises	Vocalises	Vocalises
Songs	Songs	Songs	Songs
Hours Practiced	Hours Practiced	Hours Practiced	Hours Practiced

Date:	Date:	Date:	Lesson Day
Vocalises	Vocalises	Vocalises	Vocalises
Songs	Songs	Songs	
Hours Practiced	Hours Practiced	Hours Practiced	Total Hours Practiced

Observations, Questions, Concerns, and Notes

Music hath
charms to
soothe a
savage breast,
to soften
rocks, or bend
a knotted oak.

—William
Congreve, *The
Mourning Bride*

Posture:

Breathing:

Listening:

Sight-reading:

Information about songs / arias:

Songs memorized:

Practice Sheet

Date:	Date:	Date:	Date:
Vocalises	Vocalises	Vocalises	Vocalises
Songs	Songs	Songs	Songs
Hours Practiced	Hours Practiced	Hours Practiced	Hours Practiced

Date:	Date:	Date:	Lesson Day
Vocalises	Vocalises	Vocalises	Vocalises
Songs	Songs	Songs	
Hours Practiced	Hours Practiced	Hours Practiced	Total Hours Practiced

Observations, Questions, Concerns, and Notes

The life of
man to every
part has need
of harmony
and rhythm.

—Plato, *Laws*

Posture:

Breathing:

Listening:

Sight-reading:

Information about songs / arias:

Songs memorized:

Practice Sheet

Date:	Date:	Date:	Date:
Vocalises	Vocalises	Vocalises	Vocalises
Songs	Songs	Songs	Songs
Hours Practiced	Hours Practiced	Hours Practiced	Hours Practiced

Date:	Date:	Date:	Lesson Day
Vocalises	Vocalises	Vocalises	Vocalises
Songs	Songs	Songs	
Hours Practiced	Hours Practiced	Hours Practiced	Total Hours Practiced

Observations, Questions, Concerns, and Notes

I believe art is born, not of "I can", but of "I must"!

—Arnold Schoenberg, *Problems in Teaching Art, Musikalisches Taschembuch, II* (1910)

Posture:

Breathing:

Listening:

Sight-reading:

Information about songs / arias:

Songs memorized:

Practice Sheet

Date:	Date:	Date:	Date:
Vocalises	Vocalises	Vocalises	Vocalises
Songs	Songs	Songs	Songs
Hours Practiced	Hours Practiced	Hours Practiced	Hours Practiced

Date:	Date:	Date:	Lesson Day
Vocalises	Vocalises	Vocalises	Vocalises
Songs	Songs	Songs	
Hours Practiced	Hours Practiced	Hours Practiced	Total Hours Practiced

Observations, Questions, Concerns, and Notes

I like an aria
to fit a singer
as perfectly as
a well-tailored
suit of clothes.

—Wolfgang
Amadeus
Mozart, *Letter,*
(1778)

Posture:

Breathing:

Listening:

Sight-reading:

Information about songs / arias:

Songs memorized:

Practice Sheet

Date:	Date:	Date:	Date:
Vocalises	Vocalises	Vocalises	Vocalises
Songs	Songs	Songs	Songs
Hours Practiced	Hours Practiced	Hours Practiced	Hours Practiced

Date:	Date:	Date:	Lesson Day
Vocalises	Vocalises	Vocalises	Vocalises
Songs	Songs	Songs	
Hours Practiced	Hours Practiced	Hours Practiced	Total Hours Practiced

Observations, Questions, Concerns, and Notes

I see you have
a singing face.

—John
Fletcher, *The
Wild-Goose
Chase, II ,ii,*
(1621)

Posture:

Breathing:

Listening:

Sight-reading:

Information about songs / arias:

Songs memorized:

Practice Sheet

Date:	Date:	Date:	Date:
Vocalises	Vocalises	Vocalises	Vocalises
Songs	Songs	Songs	Songs
Hours Practiced	Hours Practiced	Hours Practiced	Hours Practiced

Date:	Date:	Date:	Lesson Day
Vocalises	Vocalises	Vocalises	Vocalises
Songs	Songs	Songs	
Hours Practiced	Hours Practiced	Hours Practiced	Total Hours Practiced

Observations, Questions, Concerns, and Notes

Our business
is emotion and
sensitivity —
to be the
sensors of the
human race.

—Janet Baker,
interview in
The Observer,
(1982)

Posture:

Breathing:

Listening:

Sight-reading:

Information about songs / arias:

Songs memorized:

Practice Sheet

Date:	Date:	Date:	Date:
Vocalises	Vocalises	Vocalises	Vocalises
Songs	Songs	Songs	Songs
Hours Practiced	Hours Practiced	Hours Practiced	Hours Practiced

Date:	Date:	Date:	Lesson Day
Vocalises	Vocalises	Vocalises	Vocalises
Songs	Songs	Songs	
Hours Practiced	Hours Practiced	Hours Practiced	Total Hours Practiced

Observations, Questions, Concerns, and Notes

Music, the greatest good that mortals know,
And all of heaven we have below.

—Joseph Addison,
Song for St Cecilia's Day

Posture:

Breathing:

Listening:

Sight-reading:

Information about songs / arias:

Songs memorized:

Practice Sheet

Practice Sheet

Date:	Date:	Date:	Date:
Vocalises	Vocalises	Vocalises	Vocalises
Songs	Songs	Songs	Songs
Hours Practiced	Hours Practiced	Hours Practiced	Hours Practiced

Date:	Date:	Date:	Lesson Day
Vocalises	Vocalises	Vocalises	Vocalises
Songs	Songs	Songs	
Hours Practiced	Hours Practiced	Hours Practiced	Total Hours Practiced

Let but thy
voice engender
with the string
And angels
will be born,
while thou dost
sing.

—Robert
Herrick, *Upon
Her Voice*

Observations, Questions, Concerns, and Notes

Posture:

Breathing:

Listening:

Sight-reading:

Information about songs / arias:

Songs memorized:

Practice Sheet

Practice Sheet

Date:	Date:	Date:	Date:
Vocalises	Vocalises	Vocalises	Vocalises
Songs	Songs	Songs	Songs
Hours Practiced	Hours Practiced	Hours Practiced	Hours Practiced

Date:	Date:	Date:	Lesson Day
Vocalises	Vocalises	Vocalises	Vocalises
Songs	Songs	Songs	
Hours Practiced	Hours Practiced	Hours Practiced	Total Hours Practiced

Order Form

Quantity	Item	Price	Total
	Releasing The Inner Voice and CD	$29.95*	

*1-10 copies of the book and tape @$29.95 each
20% discount for more than 10 copies ($23.95 each)
(Tennessee Residence add 9.25% sales tax) $_____

Shipping and handling $4.00 1-3 books and CD's
more than three books $1.00 per book and CD $_____

Total: $_____

Make check payable to: ISI Publishing

Call ISI Publishing for special discounts for large orders and for teachers and coaches ordering for their students. (615) 373-3588

Ships to: _____ name

          _____ address

          _____ city/state/zip

Mail order form with check to: Purchase Order # _____

ISI Publishing   or: Email your order with purchase order
PO Box 431   number to: **orders@impactseminars.com**
Brentwood, TN 37024-0431